C000245510

Adnan Syed

The Truth Behind The *Serial* Case
and the Murder of Hae Min Lee

Roger Harrington

Introduction

In 2014, the story of a decade-old murder of a high school senior in Baltimore, Maryland became a sensation when the podcast *Serial* finally told the story of Hae Min Lee, a popular student at Woodlawn High School who was murdered in January 1999.

The little-known story was finally able to receive the national attention it deserved. The story of the horrific murder of a young girl with a promising future captivated 100 million listeners and generated an interest in the case. This growing interest and public awareness resulted in a new trial and previously ignored evidence to be taken into account.

At the center of the case is the young man proven guilty and tried for the murder of his ex-girlfriend, Adnan Syed. Syed has now spent over half is life in prison and possibly for nothing and has proclaimed his innocence the entire time.

Like many cases, this one is surrounded in doubt, mistrial, unreliable stories, and unreliable evidence which sent a potentially innocent man to prison for almost twenty years.

Adnan and Hae

The entire story of Adnan Syed and his potential involvement in the murder of Hae Lee can be attributed to accounting for only twenty-one minutes of his time in January 1999. Where was he from 2:15 to 2:360 p.m on what he described was "just another ordinary day?"

Sarah Koenig, host of the *Serial* podcast states in the opening episode how difficult it can be to account for one's time and how, such as in the case of Adnan Syed how it can lead to being implicated and charged with a crime. The question attempted to be answered in regards to this case include: what happened the day of January 13, 1999? Where exactly was Adnan Syed? Who really killed Hae Min Lee?

Koenig was a former reporter for the *Baltimore Sun* newspaper was contacted by Rabia Chaudry, a lawyer and family friend of the Syed's to review Adnan's case. Chaudry is currently working to overturn Adnan's murder conviction.

After reviewing all the evidence and facts in the case, it is obvious someone involved is lying as the evidence and stories don't add up to what happened. Sarah Koenig and now millions of listeners are trying to find out who is lying.

Both Hae Lee and Adnan were well-liked at their high school. They both have been described as "goodie two shoes." Adnan played football and ran track, Hae played lacrosse and field hockey. Both were very smart and in a magnet program at

Woodlawn High. Adnan had plans to attend the University of Maryland after graduation.

Adnan was a part-time ETM and Hae worked at a local Lenscrafters. He had scored the highest on the Maryland EMT test in his class. They were responsible, excellent students, full of promise, and destined for a bright future. The on-again-off-again couple were the last people anyone would suspect to be involved in such a shocking crime.

Hae's death and Adnan's eventual imprisonment for the crime were a major shock to those who knew them, but there was a dark side behind the facade of high school perfection.

The Syed family were strict, traditional Muslims and active in their local mosque. Adnan himself was a practicing Muslim and had strong religious convictions. Adnan's Pakistani immigrant parents forbid him from dating, drinking, smoking, sex, etc. He hid his relationship with Hae and his other various forbidden activities from his family out of fear.

The strict Muslim family would also not have liked their son being romantically involved with a girl outside his own race and religion as Hae was a South Korean immigrant. Adnan was also a known marijuana user, something else his parents would have frowned upon.

The secrecy of Adnan's relationship with Lee and his hidden behaviors did not look good for him in the context of being a murder suspect. Friends of both Adnan and Hae stated they had a stereotypical, normal high school relationship.

During the trial, the state painted Adnan as a jealous, possessive boyfriend who snapped and killed his former girlfriend in an fit of rage. Koenig notes that those she interviewed about Adnan never mentioned him being violent or possessive of Hae.

Their friends did mention how their relationship was often dramatic and that they would break up and get back together frequently. The couple would page and call one another several times a day, so their relationship could be described as being "clingy."

A friend interviewed for Serial under the pseudonym "Debbie" said that "Adnan was very over protective of Hae. He never made her sustain from seeing her friends but he did suggest she spent more time with him. He wanted to know where she was going, when she was going, who was she with, almost like he was her father."

Although the relationship between Adnan and Hae didn't appear to be abusive nor did anyone interviewed mention Adnan's possessiveness, a passage in Hae's diary tells a different story. An expert of Hae's diary posted on a blog said the following: "The second thing is the possessiveness. Independence (indiscernible). I'm a very independent person. I rarely rely on my parents. Although I love him, it's not like I need him. I know I'll be just fine without him, and I need some time for myself and (indiscernible) other than him. How dare he get mad at me for planning to hang with Aisha (Hae's best friend)?"

Some have criticized *Serial* for leaving out this information in order to make the case appear to be an wrongful conviction in order to please the media and millions of listeners. Wrongful conviction cases bring up many emotions for people and have become a hot button controversial issue in the past several years due to the exposure of the case and the Steven Avery case presented in *Making A Murderer*.

It also wouldn't be helpful for the producers of *Serial* to have produced the podcast and told the story from this angle as Sarah Koenig was in contact with Adnan and received most of her information from the source.

There was also an incident revealed where Hae hide from Adnan once in a classroom at school and had a teacher lie for her when Adnan came looking for her. This was also left out of *Serial*. It is unclear if leaving out these instances was done on purpose in order to sway the entire story in favor of Adnan. Considering how the podcast was produced, it seems to be that way. It is also unknown if the producers of *Serial* even knew about these claims, although it is likely the producers were aware of it as a simple web search can find not-so-hidden information.

The fact Adnan and Hae had to keep their relationship secret caused some strain between the two. This is something Hae mentioned in her diary on numerous occasions. Even though Adnan was dating, drinking, and having sex, all things his religion and strict parents forbade, he still wanted to be a good Muslim.

Hae felt Adnan was going to leave her because of his devotion to Islam. She also mentioned this in her diary and felt eventually his religion and family would come between them. During a phone interview between Sarah Koenig and Adnan, she mentioned a time when he allegedly referred to Hae as a "devil", meaning she was an evil driving him away from his religion.

Adnan denied the name calling in a serious manner, claiming he probably did it as a joke. However, this did seem to bother Hae as she wrote about it in her diary.

Their friends also knew about having to keep their relationship secret and the pressure it put on them. Adnan himself said that when the police came to his house to question him after Hae's disappearance he was more terrified of his parents finding out about his romantic relationship with Hae more so than being questioned by the police.

Another time, Adnan and Hae went to a school dance together without his parents knowing. However, in their small Muslim community someone found out Adnan was at the dance with a girl and told his parents. They then showed up at the school dance and confronted him. When Hae realized what was happening This incident was a turning point in the relationship for Hae. As she had stated in her diary, she was independent and didn't like his parents interfering with their relationship.

Despite her fears about their relationship ending because of Adnan's religion, it didn't happen that way. Instead, Hae ended their relationship because she developed feelings for a co-worker, Don. Soon after Hae broke up with Adnan, she and Don started dating. Surprisingly, Don was not a suspect in the murder. There is little to know about Don except that he worked at Lenscrafters with Hae.

Don's alibi for the afternoon of January 13 was that he was working. Another bit of information Serial left out was that the supervisor who gave police the alibi was Don's own mother who worked at the store with her son and Hae. Don also claimed he was working at a different Lenscrafters location the day Hae disappeared.

When his employment records were subpoenaed by Adnan's defense team, they showed he had worked at the other location but it was not on January 13. This immediately makes Don suspicion but he still was a major suspect. Many theorize that Don was responsible for Hae's murder and that his own mother doctored his employment records to secure an alibi.

The police instead focused solely on Adnan after receiving an anonymous phone call from a young man (who is believed to have been a fellow Woodlawn student) advising police to "check into the ex-boyfriend, Adnan Syed).

Overall, Adnan Syed was not viewed as the type of person who would kill another, especially Hae who many believed he truly loved. Adnan was very caring, helpful, and kind. However, others painted another picture.

One of the most incriminating pieces of evidence against Adnan's character is the fact that he stole money from the collection plate at his mosque. Witnesses saw this happen on numerous occasions. In an interview with Sarah Koenig Adnan admitted to stealing several hundred dollars from the donation plate during the summer between seventh and eighth grade.

Some indicated that this is a dead giveaway for Adnan being a sociopath, a word that has been thrown around Adnan for years. The theft is an isolated event and not at all indicative of any future behavior considering Adnan's age at the time of the thefts. Several people interviewed for *Serial* seemed to think this was enough to paint Adnan as a criminal and a future murderer.

Even almost twenty years later and evidence proving the contrary those who knew Adnan and Hae are still in shock about the murder of their friend and classmate. Everyone interviewed for *Serial* stated that "the Adnan they knew" could not have been responsible for the death of Hae. Those who knew Adnan were quick to defend him, except one crucial witness and perhaps the most important person in the entire case, Jay Wilds.

The Investigation and Jay's Stories

Jay Wilds was a friend of Adnan's, although they both stated they were not close friends but more like friendly acquaintances, in this case translates to Jay was Adnan's drug dealer. Jay was known to deal marijuana but denied ever dealing in harder drugs, which might have been one of the many lies Jay told police during the investigation.

A former homicide detective hired by Serial to review the case for any information that the writers, researchers, and producers might have missed said the case was "a mess".

The detective also stated that this case was not normal in comparison to similar murder cases, meaning that it is rare for a case with so few people involved to have so many inconsistencies and holes. As a result of these inconsistencies, this case is extremely difficult to follow and conclude.

Jay is the most polarizing and mysterious aspect of the entire case. The known "criminal element of Woodlawn", as Jay referred to himself in a police interview, Jay is believed to have been contacted by Adnan due to his lifestyle. Others have mentioned that "Jay was the person you'd call if you needed help with something like hiding a body."

Much like Adnan, many who knew Jay were surprised by his involvement in the murder. Unlike Adnan, there were others who weren't as surprised When asked about Jay during Serial, people who knew him offered various accounts including "goofy", "artistic", "beautifully unconventional."

Others were not surprised Jay was involved. A former co-worker said Jay liked to brag

Jay was a year older than Adnan and Hae and had also attended Woodlawn High School and graduated the previous year. What Jay told police and prosecutors is what the state used to build their case against Adnan, and it might have been a lie.

The context of Jay's various stories cannot fully be understand until one has a grasp on the events of January 13, 1999, although there are various accounts of what actually happened depending on the source.

On that cold, Wednesday afternoon Hae Lee was reported after she didn't pick up her younger cousin from school around 3:15

p.m., something she did every day. She had been seen by several witnesses leaving Woodlawn High School that day.

According to the first testimony given by Jay, he stated Adnan was angry at Hae for having recently broken up with him. Hae had also started dating someone else, an older man named Don who worked at Lenscrafters with her.

Jay Wilds told police Adnan was very angry at Hae Lee and that Adnan told him, "I'm going to kill that bitch." According to Jay, Adnan did just that. Depending on the which version of the story is being told by Jay, Adnan either had been planning to kill Hae for several weeks (they had broken up at the end of December) and he'd told him about his murderous plan prior to January 13. Or Adnan's anger and frustration about losing Hae boiled over to where he couldn't take it and murdered her.

During Jay's first police questioning, he said he and Adnan had gone to a local mall during Adnan's lunch period to buy a gift for Jay's girlfriend, Stephanie as January 13 was her birthday. During the trip to the mall is when Jay told police Adnan said he was planning on killing Hae.

Jay had borrowed Adnan's phone and car to go to the mall, meaning he had Adnan's car and phone for most of the afternoon, including during the state's timeline of the murder. This is important later when cellphone records are investigated. This detail also points to Jay potentially having killed Hae instead of Adnan.

According to Jay's first interview, Adnan called him at 3:40 p.m using a payphone in a Best Buy parking lot and asked Jay to meet him. Jay drove Adnan's car to the Best Buy where he showed Jay Hae Lee's dead body in the trunk of her car.

This story implies that Hae drove Adnan and they ended up at Best Buy where he strangled her in her car. School was released at 2:15 and the state later said Hae was dead by 2:36.

It should be noted here that earlier in the day witnesses claimed Adnan asked Hae for a ride after school as he had let Jay borrow his car that morning. Even after their breakup, Hae and Adnan remained friends. They had almost every class together and had a large group of mutual friends so this wasn't unusual for them to be interacting.

When asked about this, Adnan couldn't remember if he had or not but mentions that Hae picked up her younger cousin everyday after school and knew she wouldn't be able to. The state believed that Adnan asked Hae for a ride as a way to get in the car with her in order to kill her. Adnan claimed he most likely wouldn't have asked Hae for a ride because he knew she picked up her younger cousin every day. Several of their friends reported that they overheard Adnan ask Hae for a ride after school.

Hae was also the manager of the Woodlawn wrestling team and that had a match scheduled after school which Hae had to attend. This also means that she wouldn't have given him a ride home because she had something planned that day.

One theory is that Hae was actually planning to go meet her new , Don right after school before the wrestling match which is why she was in a hurry to leave. There were witnesses who did see Hae leave the school's campus.

This is also important for the state's timeline of when the murdered occurred. One of Hae's friends interviewed for Serial said that Hae could not have been dead at 2:36 because she'd been talking to Hae then about the wrestling team. Other witnesses said to have seen Hae at the school around the same time.

What Adnan initially told police greatly differs from Jay's account. According to Adnan he went straight to the Woodlawn Public Library right across the street from the high school to check his email. After visiting the library from 2:15 to 3:30, he believed he went to track practice but when he was questioned by the police four weeks later, he wasn't sure.

The track practice was supposedly from 3:30 to either 4:30 or 5:00. His track coach was contacted by police and said he did not take attendance that day and cannot prove Adnan was at practice. It was during this time that Hae Lee was murdered.

Adnan being at the library during that time should have been vital to the defense. A potential alibi witness, Asia McClain wrote an affidavit in March 1999 claiming she saw Adnan at the library and had a conversation with him.

Asia's testimony was never mentioned to any lawyers either for the prosecution of the defense. Her role in the case has been controversial from the start. Adnan was not aware of the signed affidavit claiming Asia saw him in the library until she'd sent him a letter telling him about the document while he was already in jail.

When Asia was contacted by Serial and by a private investigator hired by Rabia Chaudry to find her, she refused to participate and talk to anyone. She has since changed her mind and has written a book about her experience and appears to be enjoying her spotlight.

Those who have studied the case believe that Asia's testimony was suppressed in an effort for the police to close the case. In general, the police face immense amounts of pressure from the families of victims, the media, and lawyers to solve murder case. This is attributed to many wrongful convictions and eventual mistrials.

In 2016, two classmates of Adnan and Asia's at Woodlawn High came forward stating Asia's about seeing Adnan in the library was a lie.

The Baltimore Sun reported the story in August 2016, a month after Adnan was granted a new trial by a Baltimore judge. The classmates, two sisters who have wished to remain anonymous contacted Asia McClain in 2014 after the Serial podcast aired and confronted her.

One of the sisters stated, "she (Asia) believed so much in Adnan's innocence that she would make up a lie to prove he couldn't have done it Both my sister and I (more so my sister) argued with Asia about how serious this situation was. She just said that it wouldn't hurt anything — that if he was truly guilty, then he would be convicted. I'm not sure what can come of this information but I felt I had to let someone know."

The sisters also said that Asia inserted herself into the story because she'd heard about it at school. They also wrote McClain a Facebook message and said, "(Adnan) never told anyone, the police or his attorney to pursue you in the investigation because he knew you were full of it — he knew it never happened."

They recalled an incident at school shortly after Adnan was arrested for Hae Lee where Asia stated she wanted to help Adnan and was willing to lie to do it. One of the sisters recalled a her fighting about this with Asia during one of the their classes in which another person had to intervene.

In her interview with Sarah Koenig, Asia states that she "would not have remembered if not for the snow. It was the first snow of the year." Records indicate that there was no snow on January 13, 1999 in Baltimore but an ice storm the next day. The first snow of the year was actually a week earlier on January 8. Asia either mixed up the dates or was lying.

While it still is not known if Adnan was actually in the library that day, McClain's recent behavior towards the whole ordeal appears to fall in line with what the sister's are claiming. It could also mean that Adnan told Rabia Chauncy about Asia's claim of seeing him in the library as a potential alibi. Only he did not tell Rabia about Asia's letters until after his trial which signals to him using it as a last resort.

It is also believed Adnan's family conspired with Asia to write the letters claiming she was with him in the library. This is very unlikely considering the circumstances. Asia also stated several times she would only testify to Adnan if she knew for a fact he was innocent.

If Asia is telling the truth, it means that there is an alibi for Adnan. However, Sarah Koenig when to the library and discovered the security tapes of the library that day were long recorded over and there were no other records indicating Adnan being in the library.

When Sarah Koenig told Adnan she talked to Asia McClain who still stands by her story, he didn't seem phased by their conversation. Adnan implied that it was too late to use Asia's alibi and that no one would believe him after all of these years.

When Koenig told Rabia Chauncy about her conversation with Asia she broke down in tears. Some have noted the differences in their reactions as troubling and possibly suggest either Adnan conspired with Asia to have her write the letters or that Rabia had something to do with the letters as well.

Also the fact that Adnan's defense lawyer Christine Gutierrez never used Asia as a witness suggests that she knew Adnan had Asia write the letters. However Gutierrez was also later disbarred in 2001 for mishandling evidence so there is not much credence to this theory. Gutierrez died in 2004.

Since there is no proof besides Asia McClain's story that Adnan was in the library at the time Hae Lee was murdered the Asia letters as they are known are not exactly reliable.

If Adnan wasn't in the library at the time of Hae's murder, where was he? This goes back to Jay's various stories. While Adnan could have been at track practice then, Jay states that he dropped at Adnan at track practice at 4:30 after dumping Hae Lee's car at the I-70 Park and Ride.

After track practice, Jay picked Adnan up at 6:45 and then went to a nearby McDonald's around 7:00. He says he and Adnan went back to the I-70 Park and Ride to get Hae's car which Adnan drove to Leakin Park where Jay says they buried her body in the woods.

They drove around some more and dumped Hae's car in a residential area. Jay says they threw away her belongings and the shovel they used to dig the hole in a dumpster at the Westview Mall. Then, they went to 7/11 and Adnan dropped Jay off at home.

This is where someone else comes into the story-Jenn Pusateri. Jenn was a friend of Jay's and his girlfriend, Stephanie. Jenn and Stephanie were in a sorority together at the University of Maryland. If the stories to be believed, Jay was possibly cheating on Stephanie with Jenn. In a police interview, Jay alluded to not being faithful to Stephanie but offered no further details. Stephanie was also one of Adnan and Hae's best friends.

Earlier in the day before meeting with Adnan, Jay spent most the day with Jenn which she also claimed in her police questioning. Jenn, was friends with Stephanie but not with Adnan and Hae. There is a theory that Hae caught Jay and Jenn together and threatened to tell Stephanie so Jay and Jenn killed Hae to hide it.

Another possibly is that Jenn and Jay conspired together to kill Hae after she caught them together. Grouped into the possibility of Jenn and Jay having killed Hae is that either one of them killed Hae alone and Jay framed Adnan.

In his second police interview, Jay mentioned spending more time with Jenn and during the first interview. During the second interview, Jay says Adnan told him earlier that day that he was planning to kill Hae. In both versions of his story, Jay confesses to telling Jenn about Hae's murder.

During the trial Christine Gutierrez proposed this theory to insinuate Jay was cheating on Stephanie. It is speculated that sometime during the trial, Adnan mentioned to Gutierrez that Stephanie's parents didn't like Jay and used this again him in court. In a tape of the trial, Gutierrez is heard accusing Jay of "stepping out" on his girlfriend as a way to defame him.

The second version of Jay's story is where the claim about Best Buy shows up. Jay told police Adnan called him and asked him to come pick him up at Best Buy where he showed Jay Hae's dead body in the trunk of her car. This is one of the beloved locations of the murder. Rumors also circulated that Adnan had strangled Hae in the parking lot of the Woodlawn Library across from the high school.

This was in the middle of the afternoon in a busy part of town. Why would someone commit a murder in a very public place in the middle of the day, let alone show someone a dead body?

The Best Buy parking lot is where the state believed the murder took place regardless of who was committing the murder. Jay did not mention the events at Best Buy until his second police interview. He also mentioned it at the trial and during his second testimony. During Jenn's interview, she also mentioned that Jay told her the murder happened at Best Buy and that is where Adnan showed Jay Hae's body.

If the murder supposedly took place at Best Buy, why were there no other witnesses? This was a very busy store and a heavily populated part of town, someone would have seen this happen. There also were no security cameras at Best Buy at the time so if this did happen in the parking lot there wouldn't be any footage.

One aspect about the Best Buy story that was brought up during Serial was that someone would most likely not forget where they saw a dead body in the trunk of a car. Even though Jay was involved in some illegal activity, according to a former co-worker he wasn't the type to be involved in a murder. Serial argued seeing something that shocking and traumatic would have a lasting impression on someone and they would have most likely remembered where they saw such a thing.

Where did the Best Buy story come from? Why did Jay suddenly bring that into the narrative? At first, Jay told police that Adnan had shown him Hae's body in the trunk of her car at a strip mall on Edmonson Avenue.

He later admitted to police that he'd lied about seeing Hae's body in the trunk on Edmonson Avenue. When the police asked him why he lied, Jay said "I thought there were cameras at Best Buy." This should be a tell and this is why the state used Best Buy as the murder location in their case against Adnan. The fact Jay said he was worried about cameras obviously points to something related to the murder happening at Best Buy. It could be inferred that Jay changed his story and possibly told the truth because the police did not arrest him or hold him after his first questioning.

During her questioning, Jenn also mentioned Best Buy. She told police Jay told her Adnan told him he had killed Hae at Best Buy. Both

Jenn and Jay claim that Jay was at her house until around 3:40, which is when Adnan supposedly called Jay from a payphone at Best Buy and told him to come pick him up.

On April 20, 1999, police interviewed a friend of Adnan's, Ja'uan. This interview occurred seven weeks after Adnan was arrested. Ja'uan told police that he and Adnan had gone to the Best Buy parking lot on several occasions to smoke weed. He told said that Adnan told him and he and Hae would also have sex in one of their cars in the Best Buy parking lot.

Clearly, Adnan was familiar and comfortable with the structure of the Best Buy parking lot, which in hindsight does not look good for him. Both Jay and Ja'uan were asked by the police to draw a map of the Best

Buy parking lot and show were they smoked and where he showed Jay the body.

Their drawings showed Adnan having parked in a secluded area surrounded by various trees on both occasions. This similar detail shows that it is conceivable that something did happen in this parking lot. Adnan's cellphone records also show that a cellphone tower pinged near Best Buy, proving that the phone was at Best Buy or close enough to have pinged that tower.

Jay also stated in both his versions of what happened that he and Adnan had dumped Hae's car in a residential lot. He maintains that he was driving Adnan's car and Adnan was driving Hae's. Jay also took police to Hae's car.

The timeline and when the investigation says when Hae was murdered is widely disputed. Adnan himself and other former Woodlawn students said that it would be impossible for one to leave Woodlawn and make it over to Best Buy at that time of day in just twenty-one minutes.

Adnan and others mentioned that when school was released for the day, you didn't get to leave at exactly 2:15. There were 1,500 other students leaving at the same time as well as having to wait for school buses to clear in the parking lot. Adnan told Sarah Koenig that is took him about fifteen to twenty minutes to leave school each day when he was driving.

For an episode of Serial, Koenig and one of the show's producers made the drive themselves from Woodlawn High School to the Best Buy at the time of the school's release. Koenig and the producer were able to make the drive from the school to the store in traffic in exactly twenty-two minutes. Only one minute shy of the state's timeline of the murder, meaning that the timeline was possible.

When Adnan was told about, he was shocked and despondent. Some might take his reaction as meaning that he's been caught even though he maintains his innocence although he still either cannot or won't account for his whereabouts during the time of the murder.

If Jay was at Best Buy at the time of the murder, this points to him having killed Hae more so than Adnan. This is a theory many have considered. Based on Jay's ever-changing testimony and stories, his criminal background, and reputation he very well could have murdered Hae and then framed Adnan. However, Jay barely knew Hae and would have no motive for her murder. The lack of motive makes this highly unlikely but still in the realm of possibility.

There are very few similarities between the story's Jay told the police and what Adnan told police including going to the mall with Adnan, leaving Hae's car at the Park and Ride, picking Adnan up at track practice, Adnan letting Jay borrow his car and phone, Jay having been at Jenn's house, and going to Leakin Park and burying Hae.

One of these similarities is both Jay and Adnan having gone to the house of a friend of his and Jenn's (more so Jenn's but Jay appeared to have known her well enough to go to her house), "Cathy." Both Jay and

Adnan told police they were at Cathy's house around 6:00 to 6:15 p.m on the night of January 13. They said that they went to Cathy's to smoke some more weed.

Cathy was one of Jenn's best friends and it seemed that she knew Jay well enough to let him into her apartment. There are conflicting reports with this story which point to Cathy not being good friends with Jay but that maybe she and/or her boyfriend who was present at the apartment at the time had bought weed from him before.

Cathy, who did not want to be identified by her real name, which is now believed to be Kristi agreed to be interviewed for Serial. Not much is known about Cathy other than she is the daughter of a homicide detective in a town near Baltimore. She stated that Jay randomly appeared at her house on January 13 with Adnan, who she did not know.

She mentioned how Jay seemed nervous and was more "chatty" than usual even though he was an outgoing person. Cathy also mentioned Adnan's strange behavior. She said she was "shocked" when Jay showed up when he did.

It was at Cathy's apartment where Officer Adcock from the Baltimore Police Department called Adnan looking for Hae. Around the same time, Hae's brother also called Adnan on his cellphone looking for his sister. Cathy said that Adnan started to panic and grow paranoid (most likely from the massive amounts of marijuana he'd smoked that day) after the police called him.

Adnan, Jay, and Cathy all have said that Jay and Adnan left her house around 7:00 that night. This is one fact that has never been disputed, Jay even mentioned it during the trial. In the story Jay told at the trial, he said that he had gone to Cathy's at 5:30, left to pick Adnan up at track practice at 5:55, he arrived at track practice at 6:10, then he and Jay headed back to Cathy's, and finally left around 7:00 to retrieve Hae's car from the Park and Ride, then to Leakin Park where they buried her body.

It has been suggested that perhaps Cathy recalled the wrong day. This does seem unlikely as she suggested Jay didn't randomly stop by her apartment on a regular basis; she would probably remember the day Jay showed up and brought a stranger who was contacted by the police, especially if the stranger in her living room was soon arrested for murder.

While it seems obvious Jay and Adnan went to Cathy's house to smoke weed, there is more likely another explanation. Neither Jay or Adnan ever explain why they went to Cathy's when they did. It has been suggested that going to see Cathy was an effort by Jay to secure his own alibi.

Comparing this to the other stories Jay told, using Cathy as an alibi wouldn't make any sense as Jay already told police that he had seen Hae's body and been with Adnan at the time of the murder. Why exactly would he go to Cathy's?

A Reddit post suggested that since Cathy's father was a homicide detective, Jay was going to try to vet her and find out where bodies were buried in the city, as he and Adnan still had not buried Hae at this point in the narrative. It is possibly Cathy might not have even known that information. The post suggested the main reason Jay went to Cathy's was to secure an alibi for himself as Cathy was the most upstanding person in Jay's circle of friends.

Clearly, Jay or Adnan did not think this through as the state's timeline already had Hae as being dead by this point. When Jay and Adnan went to Cathy's Hae's body had to have been in the trunk of Adnan's car. Looking back, it appears both selfish and foolish of Jay to drag Cathy and her boyfriend into the narrative.

Cathy and her boyfriend luckily were only witnesses and were not further involved. Another connection to the Cathy story goes back to Jenn. Jay said in both of his police interviews that he told Jenn Adnan killed Hae then they both went back to Cathy's house after he had helped Adnan bury the body.

Jay either went back to Cathy's to further supply an alibi for himself and Jenn, who according to Jay picked him up from Cathy's and drove him to dump his clothes in a dumpster behind the Westview Mall and helped him wipe fingerprints off the shovels Jay and Adnan used to bury Hae.

Being with Cathy would also have worked as an alibi for Jenn since by being with Jay and driving him to dump his clothes and tampering with the evidence made her an accessory to the crime. Even though Jay maintained he was with Jenn and Cathy's for the remainder of the evening until he went home around 11:00, Adnan and his father's testimony, he went to McDonald's, came back home around 7:00, and drove his father to the mosque for evening prayer where he stayed until 10 or 10:30.

Unfortunately, Adnan's story doesn't end there.

More Stories, The Call Log, and the Trial

As the investigation into Hae's disappearance and murder began, more and more stories from both Jay and Adnan started to unravel.

Hae's body was not found until February 9, almost a month after she went missing and was presumably murdered. Her body was found partially buried by Mr.S (another pseudonym), a janitor at Woodlawn. Mr. S is another mysterious figure in this story.

According to Mr. S's police interview, he left work and headed home to grab a tool on his lunch break because hd didn't have the tool at work. Leakin Park was on his route between home and work, so he stopped to relieve himself in the park where he discovered Hae's body in the woods

While this sounds like a fairly inconspicuous why to stumble across a dead body, in this case it wasn't. Hae's body was buried 127 feet back into the woods and wouldn't have been easy to find. This was discussed on Serial and Mr. S is believed to have possibly been looking for the body suggesting he either knew something about Hae's murder or he was out to claim the reward money being offered by her family (Adnan also accused Jay of doing this as well).

When he was questioned by the police, Mr. S was briefly considered a suspect. Mr. S had a criminal record for various incidents of indecent exposure and was a known streaker in the neighborhood. Once, Mr. S was

streaking and called the cops to report his
own clothing stolen along with several other
bizarre instances.

Mr. S was drinking at the time he discovered
the body. Along with being a streaker, Mr. S
was a frequent drinker and confessed to
driving back to work from with house while
drinking a beer. During his questioning, the
police asked him about the type of alcohol he
usually drank as a way to tie him to some
evidence found at the burial site. A bottle of
brandy was found near Hae's body in Leakin
Park, something Mr. S told police he never
drank. This small piece of evidence cleared
Mr. S as a suspect.

It wasn't until Mr. S found the body that Jay
went to the police and told them his first
story about what happened with Adnan.
Journalist and private investigator, Ann

Brocklehurst theorized on her blog that Jay and Jenn had not planned on telling the police what they knew about Hae's murder until Mr. S talked to police after finding her body.

Brocklehurst notes that neither Jay or Jenn contacted the police with information about Hae's murder and the location of her body. She writes that she believes this happened because Mr. S might have had some connection with either Jay, Jenn, Stephanie, or someone known to Serial listeners as "the neighbor boy". This boy, who was never named was mentioned by a girl named Laura who was interviewed for the podcast.

Laura was also a student at Woodlawn. She said she never thought Adnan was guilty but doesn't think Jay was lying. She told her father that "the neighbor boy" mentioned that he had seen a dead body in the trunk of a car. Laura told Sarah Koenig that the "kid's name was Adnan." In the interview it sounded as if she were finally remembering what had happened in an "ah-ha" moment.

This was years after the fact and it is possible Laura knew about the subject of the podcast and remembers Adnan and his case. Critics online have questioned this story's legitimacy, stating that Laura would have either remembered the story or she would have looked up the podcast ahead of time and knew what was coming her way. Laura said that it seemed like the neighbor boy "was getting it (seeing the dead body) off his chest".

The neighbor boy later spoke out under the pseudonym "E" and stated that Laura made the story up. Listeners of the podcast have noted how Laura does not sound like a credible witness. It is possible she could have lied in order to get on a world-famous, widely listened to podcast.

Considering that "E" came forward and said she'd lied sounds as if he is trying to protect himself from becoming involved in the case. He was also questioned by the police and said then that the story was a lie which ended the police's lead.

There is some truth to the neighbor boy's story-it was not public knowledge yet that Hae's body was found in the trunk of a car. This proves that he got the information from either Jay, Adnan, or from someone who either knew Jay and/or Adnan. Rabia Chaudry, who knows the true identity of neighbor boy has stated that Jay and neighbor boy were childhood friends and still interact to this day. This strongly indicates that the police were able to use this information to corroborate Jay's story.

Ann Brocklehurst continues to theorize Jay grew panicked about Mr. S talking to the police. This prompted Jay to go ahead and talk to them in case Mr. S somehow was able to implicate he or Jenn into his story. There is no evidence linking Mr. S to either Jay, Jenn, "the neighbor boy", or anyone else connected to the case.

However, there is a possibly that somehow Mr. S overheard someone mention the location of a body and the reward money and went out to find it. Another online posts suggests that it is possible that Mr. S knew Jay from the pornographic video store he started working at at the end of January 1999 and that he overheard Jay mention the murder.

Based on another Serial interview with a former co-worker of Jay's named Josh this doesn't seem likely. Josh told Sarah Koenig that Jay casually mentioned how he'd been involved with the Hae's murder one night when they were working together at the video store. Josh told Sarah he was shocked and urged Jay to go to the police with the information but Jay said he couldn't because he felt someone was after him.

Josh recalled that Jay was growing increasingly paranoid by the day. He mentioned that there was a commuter parking lot across the street from the video store and one night there was a lone van sitting in the parking lot which Jay believed to have been following and watching him waiting for him to get off work and attack him. Josh also mentioned in the podcast that Jay saw the people in the van and said they were of Middle Eastern decent.

This ties back to the possibility that Adnan planned to blackmail Jay into helping him with Hae's body by threatening to turn him into the police for his drug dealing if he didn't help him bury the body. Josh said the following: "Jay seemed afraid the cops were going to figure out he was involved through fingerprints or DNA or something, but that as time went on he seemed more and more afraid of the guy who did it, that he was threatening Stephanie. It was, "you'd better keep your mouth shut or else." He says Jay told him the threats were getting more forceful."

If this is true then Josh's claims about Jay's fear and paranoia are valid. Josh was also interviewed by the police and recalled he told them that Jay had mentioned he was involved in Hae's murder. The fact that Jay mentions fingerprints and DNA suggests that he was involved. Josh's claims and Jay's fear also would explain why he threw out his clothing. If Adnan was the one who actually killed Hae, why did Jay feel the need to throw away all of his clothes?

On February 18, 1999, Baltimore Police received Adnan's cellphone records. Adnan stated that he was the main suspect from the start. He understood why considering he was the ex-boyfriend and the two had just broken up. Considering how cases like this usually go, the current significant other is usually and logically the first suspect.

Don, Hae's new boyfriend of only thirteen days (their first date was on January 1) was not even considered a suspect. He states he was questioned by police and felt that they weren't looking at him as a suspect. Sarah Koenig reported that Don was worried he would be the primary suspect considering he was her new boyfriend and that she had been with him the night before she went missing.

Although Don was not on the police's radar, avid podcast listeners have theorized that Hae had been planning on going to see Don after school. If this story is true, it puts Don with Hae at the supposed time of her death. Don does have an alibi as he was working at the time but since it was possibly provided by his mother, there are many questions that arise. Since Jay and Jenn's stories seem to have some coherence and Don doesn't fit into their narrative, nor was their any evidence of Don having been with Hae on January 13, it seems unlikely he was responsible.

On February 12, an anonymous caller tells police that Adnan might have killed Hae. The caller also mentioned Yaser, a friend of Adnan's and said he might know something. Adnan called Yaser around 7:00 the night Hae went missing. During Yaser's police interview he stated that he believed Adnan was involved in Hae's murder and points to Adnan's brother, Tanveer having been involved as well. It has been suggested that Yaser actually made the anonymous call to the police in order to confess.

Adnan was taken into police custody on February 26. The next day, Jenn went back to

the police with a lawyer and told detectives
that Jay told her Adnan killed Hae. Adnan
was formally charged with first-degree
murder and arrested on February 28, the
same date of Jay's first interview and the
same day Jay took police to Hae's car.

During Adnan's police questioning is when
the entire narrative of the case and not being
able to account for time comes into play.
Adnan was arrested and questioned over a
month after Hae's disappearance which is
why he was so difficult for him to recall
where he was and account for his time on the
afternoon of January 13.

At the beginning of Serial, Koenig mentions
how difficult it is to account for your own
time and being able to recall where you were
on a random Wednesday four weeks ago. If
Adnan could remember exactly where he

was for only twenty-one minutes on that afternoon, and there was evidence to corroborate his claims, he might be a free man.

Shockingly, Jay never served any time for his involvement in Hae's murder. His last police interview took place on April 13, 1999, which he said he had no contact with police and was living in fear until he was picked up by police on September 7, 1999 and was asked to sign an agreement to plea guilty to being an accessory to murder after the fact. Jay was eventually sentenced to two years probation for his role in the murder.

Adnan's first trial began on December 8, 1999. His family hired well-known criminal defense lawyer, Christina Gutierrez. Gutierrez was described as "a pit bull in the courtroom". She was rough, tough, very good at her job and was known to sway jurors and win cases.

At time time, Gutierrez's health started to decline. She was sick with diabetes and multiple sclerosis and her career began to suffer as a result. Gutierrez's former employees and co-workers said that she didn't realize how sick she really was and refused to stop working. Sarah Koenig found out from one of her former law clerk's that she would demand they bring her case files while she was in the hospital for a prolonged period.

Gutierrez's main strategy was to discredit Jay's various stories while she was on the stand. Adnan wasn't even questioned or cross-examined during his own trial because. Adnan said he trusted who he always called "Miss Gutierrez" as did his family and believed she would get his conviction overturned and out of jail.

Gutierrez was a former Baltimore public defender who had made partner at a defense firm and eventually started her own lucrative and successful practice. She was known to defend "impossible" cases. One of these included a man, Jamal Craig accused of abusing children at his mother's day care center. His mother, Sandra Craig was also charged. Gutierrez was able to get them both acquitted of all charges and took the case, Maryland v. Craig to the United States Supreme Court.

Adnan said "Miss Gutierrez was like a mother, father, teacher, coach, doctor, and friend in one." He said she made sure he was being taken care of while he was in jail, she made sure he received the medicine he needed and his reading glasses. Those who knew Gutierrez said she was tough but caring and wanted the best for her clients.

During the trial, the prosecutors alleged that since Adnan was Pakistani they feared he would flee the country, return to Pakistan which had no extradition laws with the United States to avoid trial and prosecution. The state was wrong as Adnan was an American citizen, something that Gutierrez re-iterated on many occasions during the trial.

One of the main pieces of evidence in the trial was Adnan's cellphone records. Since the cell records matched up with Jay's stories, the state used the records as their primary evidence against Adnan. There was also no psychical evidence linking Adnan to Hae's murder. The only thing that could be used against him was that his fingerprints were all over her car but he'd been in the car dozens of times before during their relationship. Those prints were not used in the trial based on their past together.

There was also no DNA evidence linking Adnan to Hae's murder. If there was no DNA evidence, why was Adnan found guilty of her murder? There are multiple answers to that question, but mainly Adnan was convicted based on cellphone tower evidence. That evidence has since been proven inaccurate as technology has improved and how cellphone tower pings are interpreted and read.

It seems hard to believe today, but in the relatively short time since Adnan's trial cellphones were a recent technology. The main flaw in this case is that the state used two inaccurate pieces of evidence, the cellphone records and Jay's ever-changing story about what happened.

There are two telling pieces of evidence within the cellphone records that worked against Adnan's claims. One was known as the Nisha call. Nisha was a girl Adnan had met in 1998 and had talked too and possibly dated prior to Hae. She and Adnan were good friends and talked on a regular basis.

The cellphone records indicate that someone called Nisha around 3:00 on the afternoon of January 13, thirty minutes after the state says Hae was murdered. Supposedly, Jay had Adnan's phone at this time which both he and Adnan attested to.

If Jay had the phone, why would he be calling Nisha, someone he didn't know very well? There are many theories about the Nisha call and why it is so important. One theory is that Jay had the phone and randomly called Nisha as a way to either implicate Adnan as Jay knew there was no way for him to connected to someone he didn't know, or that he called Nisha to make it look like Adnan was with him.

During the trial, Nisha testified that Adnan had called her and Jay had talked to her during the same call. She claims that the call took place from the video store where Jay worked but he didn't start working there until the end of January so the timeline doesn't match up.

Since the call showed up on Adnan's cellphone bill and the call log, that means that the phone did ring and the call was actually made. At the time AT&T had a policy that any call which rang for over thirty seconds would be billed.

The defense tried to say that Nisha got her dates confused, which is a possibility. Serial fans, Rabia Chaudry, and Sarah Koenig have attempted to solve the mystery of the phone call Koenig called "the smoking gun." It is also possible that the call was a pocket dial or that there was a voicemail from the pocket dial that lasted more than thirty seconds. Adnan stated that Nisha's number was on speed dial on his phone which would make a pocket dial more plausible.

The other evidence and the most damning based on the cellphone records is that a call was made in Leakin Park and pinged a nearby tower. This cell tower ping matching up with Jay's story and the fact that Hae's body was found in Leakin Park was disastrous to Adnan's defense. Based on the records then and when Serial producers re-examined them, it looks like the cellphone was in fact in Leakin Park.

Besides Jay's stories and the cellphone records, what else would have led the state to having convicted Adnan? According to one juror who served on the second trial, it was simply Jay's story. When she was interviewed for Serial, she said "Jay seemed believable. He seemed like a nice young man who was telling the truth." She also said something rather jarring and makes an excellent point to the discredit of Adnan. The juror said, "why would you confess to something that drastic if you didn't do it?"

Jay had nothing to gain by talking to police and providing them with some corroborated information, and had everything to lose. No one, especially a drug dealer with a family history of incarceration and one arrest under their belt would provide all that information to police.

Adnan's first trial ended in a mistrial after only three days when a juror overhead the judge call Christina Gutierrez a "liar". It is unknown what prompted the judge to call Gutierrez a liar but it is recorded in court documents. A second trial started on January 10, 2000 and ended in six weeks.

The trial ended on February 25, 2000, with Adnan being convicted of first degree murder, kidnapping, robbery, and false imprisonment. He was sentenced on June 8, 2000, to life plus thirty years.

Further Theories and Suspects

This is one of the very rare cases in which there are more theories and questions than answers. Simply put, someone either Adnan or Jay is lying. The main question is, who is lying and what is the truth?

Besides Adnan having killed Hae, there are some other suspects and theories that Serial fans and Internet sleuths have concluded where the state failed. There are many possible theories as to what happened to Hae, some are obvious such as Adnan actually killed her to the not so obvious.

One of these theories relates to Jay, as most of the events in the story do. This theory states that Jay killed Hae alone and implicated Adnan. Why would Jay kill Hae when he barely knew her, or maybe not even at all? Jay and Adnan both stated that they weren't actually good friends. If they weren't good friends, then why would Jay and Hae know one another?

It has been theorized that Hae saw Jay involved in a drug deal either on the afternoon of January 13 or in the weeks prior to and that Jay killed her to ensure her silence. This theory about the murder ties into Hae having witnessed Jay cheating on Stephanie with Jenn and that both of these events happened either on the same day or in close proximity to one another.

Another Jay theory which actually relates back to Adnan having killed Hae is that Jay was actually a police criminal informant. This would explain why the police believed

Jay's stories immediately and why the state used his story in the trial.

The Jay is an informant theory could be applied to a sketchy aspect of the trial that is often overlooked but revealed by Koenig; the state's prosecutor, Kevin Urick secured a lawyer for Jay. Jay mentioned that he asked for a public defender but was told he couldn't get one to defend him as he wasn't being charged with anything.

After that conversation, Urick supplied a pro-bono attorney to Jay. This implies that someone within the police and the state prosecutors office was clearly trying to protect Jay from the defense. There was also no court or public record of Jay's plea hearing.

One of the most outlandish theories which originated on the Serial Reddit page, which is full of web sleuths and fans connecting dots, concocting theories, and trying to solve the case is that Jenn and Stephanie killed Hae. Considering Hae and Stephanie were best friends this is very unlikely. It is also rare for women to kill one another via strangulation as this is considered a more masculine method of murder.

This theory is based on the fact that Adnan never called Stephanie, one of his best friends as well on January 13, which was her birthday. Since Adnan and Jay went shopping together for Stephanie's birthday, why would Adnan, her friend not at least call her on her birthday?

However, Adnan's call log shows that he talked to Stephanie twice on the night of

January 12. Could Adnan have told Stephanie that Hae made him mad? Could that have led to her and Jenn, who mentioned several times she didn't like Hae to kill her? While this is far-fetched, if this did happen it does make sense for Jay's involvement. If Stephanie and Jenn killed Hae, they would obviously turn to Jay to help them cover it up.

Stephanie is one of the most myserteous figures in this entire narrative. She is always on the outskirts of the story but never truly involved. An online comment on a forum about the case mentions how Stephanie appeared to stand by Jay and believe his stories and was known to have cut off contact with Adnan after Hae was discovered to have been murdered. It is possible that Stephanie knows something (either she knows Adnan or Jay killed Hae or she was somehow more involved than she originally let on) and is not talking because of that.

There is another suspect unrelated to the circle of Woodlawn High friends, a man named Roy Sharonnie Davis III. In 2004, an untested DNA kit matched Davis to a rape and strangling murder of another 18-year-old Woodlawn High School student, Jada Lambert. Lambert was murdered in May 1998, nine months before Hae went missing.

The time line of nine months is perfect amount of time for a serial killer to experience the cooling off period between murders. This makes Davis a very viable suspect. Davis also lived six miles away from Woodlawn High School and even closer to the Campfield Early Learn Center where Hae picked up her little cousins every day, so it is very possible that Davis could have been stalking Hae and planning her murder for months.

This next possible explanation goes back to Don. Don stated that when he found out Hae was missing he started to get the facts about the last time he saw her together. He said he "immediately made sure someone knew where he was (at the time of the murder and disappearance)."

This is rather cold and clinical reaction to finding out the girl you'd been dating and said to have "fallen hard for very fast" was reported missing. Don also reportedly never tried to call Hae or her family to try and find her.

It was also later found out that Don's timecard at Lenscrafters was in fact doctored. On October 4, 1999, Lenscrafters produced paperwork saying that Don had not worked on January 13, 1999 like the original paperwork and court statements claimed.

When this was discovered by Maryland state prosecutor Kevin Urick, he contacted the Lenscrafters legal team and was able to obtain copies of the paperwork saying Don hadn't worked that day. Lenscrafters soon produced "an additional time keeping record" that showed Don had worked on January 13 after all. This was never shown to Christina Gutierrez prior to the trial to aid in the defense.

The doctored paperwork and sudden document protecting an employee appearing does not look good for Don. On January 13, a friend of Hae's named Debbie said she saw Hae at school by herself outside the gym and that Hae told her she was going to see Don at the mall after school before her shift at Lenscrafters later that night and before the wrestling match she had to attend. Hae never made it to either one.

There is not much else known about Don and he has remained quite about the case with the exception of his Serial interview. Even though he hasn't been pursued by police, the evidence against Don still makes him a viable suspect in Hae's murder.

One final theory about Adnan was suggested by a forensic psychologist on Serial who suggested that it is possible Adnan did kill Hae and simply doesn't remember it due to being in a disassociate state. This would explain why he can't remember and couldn't account for certain parts of the day.

New Developments

Since Rabia Chaudry introduced this fascinating, polarizing, and often maddening case to Sarah Koenig, millions of listeners have been moved by the story enough to raise public awareness about Adnan's case.

Since Serial was recorded in 2014, several new developments have been made in the case due to the outcry to resolve the miscarriage of justice and to potentially exonerate Adnan.

In 2015, the state of Maryland held a hearing on the case in which Asia McClain reinforced her alibi story and agreed to testify in a new trial.

Prior to hearing in 2015, Adnan first appealed his case in 2012. The appeal was based on "inadequate assistance of counsel" as Christina Gutierrez did not call Asia McClain as an alibi witness. The appeal was denied in 20 13.

On February 6, 2015, the Maryland Court of Appeals approved another appeal. In November 2015, the Superior Court elected to hear out the case. Adnan's new appeal lawyer, Justin Brown has been working tirelessly and passionately on this case. Brown has secured new evidence from AT&T which proves the cell tower evidence was not valid. Brown stated, "he cell tower evidence was misleading and should have never been admitted at trial."

Another post-conviction hearing was held from February 3-9, 2106, in which Asia

McClain again testified she had talked to Adnan in the library on January 13. Despite various claims about Asia's credibility, the state still plans on using her as an alibi witness in the second trial which was granted on June 30, 2016.

The new trial was granted under the ruling that Christina Gutierrez "rendered ineffective assistance when she failed to cross-examine the state's expert regarding the reliability of cell tower location evidence." A judge then vacated Adnan's sentence.

Brown also stated tat Gutierrez used witnesses with conflicting stories and information about Adnan's whereabouts on January 13 and that none of these stories or witnesses pointed to Adnan's only clear alibi-him being in the library with Asia McClain.

The appeals court is going to focus on Asia McClain's alibi witness statement as well as updated cellphone tower technology and the validity of the records from the 1999 case.

It is not know if Jay will be contacted to testify at the re-trial. Since the trial, he has kept a low profile. In 2014, he finally spoke out and was interviewed for The Intercept, and staying on his own trend, Jay again changed the story. This time he said that "the trunk pop" that revealed Hae's body took place at his grandmother's house (where he lived at the time), and that he and Adnan buried Hae's body in Leakin Park around midnight and not at 7:00 at night like he originally told police.

In October 2016, Justin Brown requested for bail to be granted for Adnan. Baltimore City

Circuit Court Judge Martin Welch denied the request for bail on December 29, 2016.

Along with the new trial and vacated sentence, the Innocence Project Clinic at the University of Virginia Law School has requested that Maryland finally test the DNA from Hae's murder. This was spearheaded by the project leader Deirdre Enright. Students at the law school have identified several other possible suspects convicted of similar crimes in the area. Other DNA tests have been requested from related cases to see if they match Hae's.

Adnan's new trial is set to start in late 2017.

Close

The case of Adnan Syed and Have Lee's murder is special and extraordinary in the sense that there are so many inconsistencies, contradictions, and stories. It is also special and rare that a first-degree murder case is able to receive a second and fair trial with updated and accurate evidence.

These differences and ever-changing stories must have been unimaginably frustrating to police and lawyers at the time. Since the story which needed to be told has been broadcast to the world via new technology which relies an old principle, the power of compelling storytelling millions of listeners have felt the same frustration as police, the lawyers, and most importantly Adnan, his family, and Hae's family.

Even though this case is unique and we might never know the truth, the fact that people from all over the world have come together in order to help solve this case and possibly exonerate an innocent man is wonderful and a perfect example of how technology can unite people.

The most important aspect of this entire story is that justice will hopefully finally be served for Adnan and that Hae's family will finally receive some much-needed peace and closure.

23743214R00057

Printed in Great Britain
by Amazon